Answering the Call:

Seeking the King and Advancing the Kingdom

Shayla Jesse

Library of Congress Control Number: 2025914097

ISBN paperback: 979-8-9858347-4-1

ISBN ePUB: 979-8-9858347-5-8

Printed in the United States of America

Publishing Services provided by Rebel Queen

https://rebelqueen.co/
Social media: @rebelqueenbooks

I dedicate this book to the love of my life—my husband, Todd. Your passion for life, love for your family and friends, and discipline for your craft inspire me. You set an example daily in your commitment to live a life unencumbered by others' guidelines. Your personal and spiritual growth is a testament to how good Jesus is. Thank you for believing in me and supporting me as I continue to become the woman God created me to be. I am forever grateful for the way you love me.

I love you with all my heart,

Shay

"They think they are waiting on Me,
but I am waiting on them."

-God

Father, in the name of Jesus, thank You for who You are and for always being faithful to Your Word.

Thank You for Your forgiveness and grace. Most of all, thank You for Your overwhelming love.

Jeremiah 1:5 tells us how You knew each of us before You put us in our mother's womb.

Father, I pray for the woman reading this book. When You designed her life, You had the perfect plan for her. You knew who she was and who she would become. You knew every mistake and wrong turn she would take along the way. You love her so much that You sent Jesus to die so she could live in eternity with You. You have given her a purpose— to share Your unconditional love and unimaginable forgiveness with others. Thank You for the unique calling You designed for her specifically, and the grace you have provided so she can complete every assignment You have for her.

According to Hebrews 13:21, You have equipped her with everything she needs to press into You and carry out Your plan for her life. I ask that You place people in her life that You want her connected with and remove those who are destructive to the plans You have for her. Father, I ask that You guide her; that she may know You on a deeper level by seeking You above all things—like You have commanded us in Matthew 6:33. I pray You help her to align her desires with Yours so they become her own.

God, I ask that You help her gain knowledge and seek understanding so her wisdom can grow, and her faith will be made stronger. I declare, in the name of Jesus, that no weapon formed against this woman or the assignments You've given her shall prosper. When she gets distracted, overwhelmed, and frustrated, remind her that time spent with You is the cure for all things. Show her how to rely on Your power and keep her words aligned with Yours so she does not fall prey to that which is not of You. Help her step fully into the boldness of who she is because of whom she belongs to. Thank You for Your favor, protection, and power in this woman's life.

In the precious name of Jesus, I pray, amen.

Table of Contents

WHAT'S IN THIS BOOK FOR ME?

Do you feel like you are living the same day over and over again? Does it feel more like surviving than thriving? Do you feel a void inside of you as if something is missing? That longing for more, that ache that something just isn't right? It's not an ache for a specific person or opportunity, rather it exists because when God designed you, He predestined you for specific things—which your spirit longs to fulfill.

You have been called by God to use your gifts to be a light for Jesus. You will not experience true fulfillment until you seek Him, and only then will you discover your calling. Once you have said yes to Him and taken steps to fulfill your calling through the assignments He designed for you, you will experience fulfillment. God wants to reveal your gifts to you, for you to be His partner, and for you to use your gifts to advance His kingdom.

God's kingdom needs you and your gifts. Your personality, attitude, sense of humor, quirkiness, and even your physical appearance is unique to who God has called you to be and who He has called you to serve. He made you with each characteristic for a reason. The opinions of others don't factor into who God designed you to be, and you have been called regardless of what you've done in the past. As Psalm 139:14 says, you are fearfully and wonderfully made. Your calling won't just float by one day and ask you to hop on; God will reveal it to you when you seek Him. Your calling glorifies Him and helps others, and it will bless you more than any relationship or amount of money. The ache you feel is simply a lack of throne time with Him. The waves of uncertainty inside you come from wondering how God can use you. Are you ready to stop wondering and start taking steps toward what God created you for?

As you read this book, you will learn how to seek God to answer your life's calling and say yes to His assignments. You will learn how to block out opposition from others and from your real enemy. You will no longer question if you have been called, or wonder if you have gifts God can use. You will learn how to step boldly into your purpose as a woman of God. Come, Sister, it's time to seek the King and advance His kingdom. Those in need of our God-given gifts are waiting on the other side of our obedience.

TAKING MY PLACE

In the summer of 2022, I published *The Covenant Woman.* That book was birthed from the assignment God gave me to share the significance of your faith with you. Since the book launched, I have learned so much, my faith has continued to grow, and I have become more obedient to the calling God has equipped me with. Prelaunch for the book was exhilarating. As women gained knowledge in their blood-backed covenant with God, their faith was growing stronger. Each message of thanks I received for writing the book filled me with overwhelming gratitude. It was an honor to witness how God worked through my book to help women learn who they are—daughters of the King.

After that, I wasn't sure how to continue sharing it with the public. Sure, it was on Amazon, it reached number one in the new release category, and then a year later it soared in the rankings again. I also shared it on my social media here and there, and I was comfortable with selling a few books from my website each month. From time to time, I would ask God if there was anything specific He wanted me to do with the book, and He continued leading me to share my faith on social media and to send out *The Covenant Woman* email weekly.

Fast forward to early 2024. Like I do at the beginning of each year, I asked God to show me what He wanted me to do in each area of my life, including in my relationships and finances. I asked Him to lead my steps in my network marketing business, and also specifically asked Him if there was anything He wanted me to do with my assignment, *The Covenant Woman*. He didn't say anything at the time, but a few weeks later while I was fellowshipping with Him, the Holy Spirit said something I will never forget: "I want you to start using your voice and not just hide behind written words." Immediately my heart sank, and I begged, "Oh God, please don't make me do that. Lord, You know how bad I am at speaking in front of people, and how anxious it makes me." I have a history of self-sabotage when speaking in public. Years ago, I was asked to speak at a conference in Oklahoma City for my network marketing company, and as I stood on that gigantic stage, my whole body felt shaky. I remember thinking I wasn't good enough to be sharing any words of wisdom, and although I had experienced great success in my business, I hadn't experienced much growth in the months leading up to the conference. While standing on that stage, staring out at the hundreds of faces in the crowd, I kept asking myself, "What do I even have to offer these people?"

I had always been hesitant to speak and have people see my face at the same time, and looking back, I am certain that was a scheme of satan. The enemy's aim is to steal, kill, and destroy, so of course, he would want to steal my confidence and hinder God's plans, thereby waylaying my assignments. Killing the callings of God's people and stopping us from spreading the love of Jesus is always on his agenda.

Obviously, what the Holy Spirit shared with me was not what I wanted to hear, and I quickly reminded Him, "I say 'umm' dozens of times in a ten-minute speech or video, and often stutter because I get so nervous." My mind raced to those familiar, doubt-filled thoughts: "What do I even have to offer these people?" and "What will they think?" However, the words I heard next shut them down in an instant: "Shay, it's not about you, it's about the people I can touch through you." Do you want to know one of the things I love about our Heavenly Father? He can calm my whole being with just one sentence. Although I still had some nervous feelings, I experienced a shifting inside of me, and I knew I would never be the same again.

And I'm not the same. I live differently. I think differently. I speak differently. I share Him differently. I am more bold than before. I am no longer worried what people will think when He puts a message in my heart to share with others.

Before I knew it, I was standing at my kitchen window with tears streaming down my face. "Okay, Father, I will do what You have called me to do. Just tell me how." Immediately, He put opportunities in front of me that included using my voice. A bank reached out and asked me to give a devotion. I was asked to speak on a webinar about the calling of God in a Christian's life. A podcast host I didn't know wanted to interview me about my book and the significance of a Christian's faith.

Within weeks, God told me to open a TikTok Shop. Like most people, I had a TikTok, but I rarely opened the app. I had uploaded some videos in the past, but they were mainly with someone else's audio instead of my own. I thought that was an odd task for Him to ask of me, so I put it off and completed other things until God put it in my heart so strongly that I knew I had to get it done. I added the thirty copies of *The Covenant Woman* I had in stock, and posted a few videos sharing messages God spoke to me. I sold a few books, then something I wasn't expecting happened. One Sunday, orders started rolling in. It was so exciting seeing the "Congratulations, you have a new order!" notification pop up every few minutes, but my excitement wasn't for me. I was excited for the women who were about to learn how important their faith is, and I knew lives would be changed. My books sold out that day, and I was amazed.

After talking to God, I ordered more books, and this time paired each one with *The Covenant Woman* journal that is designed to accompany it. Although I trusted God, I was nervous that I spent my profit from the sales without any certainty that I would be able to sell more books. Within a week, that entire order sold out, and when it happened a third time God told me to start placing bigger orders. As those bigger orders continued to sell out in 24–48 hours,

I kept using the profits to purchase more books and journals.

Months later, I am still in awe of how God uses my voice to share messages of faith with other women. I am baffled by the number of *The Covenant Woman* books and journals that people now have in their homes. My TikTok platform has turned into something so much bigger than I could have imagined. When we are obedient and willing to do what God tells us to do, it is awe-inspiring to see the results. He used the proceeds of *The Covenant Woman* to fund this book which will touch the lives of many women with the words He put in my heart to write.

Since then, many other things have taken place, and while I've been asked to speak on a few stages, I haven't had to search for where God wants me to be. I simply said yes to Him, and He continues to provide opportunities for me to continually choose His calling on my life with each step He puts before me.

I also hosted the very first *The Covenant Woman* conference to share the importance of the callings and assignments God puts on our hearts, and it was beautiful. The other speakers spoke straight to the hearts of the women in that building, and no one left untouched or without shedding tears. Break-throughs were had and lives were touched. Saying yes to using my voice is what led me to hosting *The Covenant Woman* conference and to share that same message with you through this book. I share my story to help and inspire you to say yes to the assignments God has designed you for.

I think back to that conversation I had with God in my kitchen, and I am reminded of how greatly God can move through our yes. I could write a book longer than this one full of stories of how God has touched the lives of thousands of women through my obedience in using my voice to share what He puts in my heart. It's not me—God gets all the glory—it's my obedience that allows Him to use me for His good. I don't take any of the credit for what God is doing, but I am honored to be partnered with Him in His plans and for His glory. I have a front row seat to many of the incredible ways God touches the lives of other women and families.

For those of you who read *The Covenant Woman*, you know God showed me what my calling is and gave me the assignment of writing that book after going through an extremely difficult season. No matter who you are, difficult seasons of life are inevitable, but I believe each one of us has grown more in our relationship with Jesus through the hard seasons of life rather than when life wasn't throwing us obstacles. Think back to when you have spent the most time with God and gained wisdom on a deeper level. When did you learn who He really is? When did your mind conceive the knowing that He is not just a being in Heaven, but that He lives inside of you? When did you grasp the fullness of His enthralling goodness? In the difficult seasons when we wonder if we are going to make it through heartbreak, the grief from loss or betrayal, or the embarrassment from our mistakes, that's when we gain true knowledge of who He is, and learn to fully depend on Him. When we fall on our faces, don't know what else to do, and stop trying to do things our own way, we start to understand that we cannot and no longer desire to live life according to our will and plans.

Hard seasons present an opportunity for the birth of something beautiful because you get to make the choice for Jesus to not only be your Savior, but also to be your Lord. In these moments, you realize how important walking in His will and allowing His direction in your life is. This is when you learn how important it is to align your will with His so His desires become your own. When you make Jesus the Lord of your life, His will is no longer an option because you recognize that His will and direction keep you, protect you, and bring favor upon you, causing His will to become the desire of your heart as well.

YOU WERE BORN INTO ROYALTY

WHO DO YOU BELONG TO?

Do you know who you belong to? You belong to God. It is easy to say, "Sure, I know who God is. I have learned about Him since I was a little kid." But have you grasped the magnitude of who He is? Until you recognize the fullness of who He is, His Word will carry little weight in how you view yourself and the way you live your life. If His Word carries no weight, He will not receive the honor He deserves.

Priscilla Shirer, a world-renowned Christian author who also happens to be one of my favorite speakers, shares who God is better than I could ever express. If you are struggling to see yourself as a child of the King of kings, read these words of hers every morning until you are no longer struggling:

"He is the first and the last. The beginning and the end. He's the keeper of creation and the creator of all. He's the architect of the universe and the manager of all time. He always was, always is, always will be unmoved, unchanged, undefeated, and never undone. He was bruised but brought healing. He was pierced but eased pain. He was persecuted but brought freedom. He was dead and brings life, He is risen to bring power, and He reigns to bring peace. The world can't understand Him. Armies can't defeat Him. Schools can't explain Him, and leaders, they can't ignore Him. Herod couldn't kill Him. Nero couldn't crush Him. The new age cannot replace Him, and Oprah cannot explain Him away! You remind yourself that He is light, He is love, He is longevity, and He is the Lord. He is goodness and kindness and faithfulness, and He is God. He is holy and righteous and powerful and pure. His ways are right, His Word eternal, His will unchanging, and His mind is on us. He's our Savior, our guide, our peace, our joy, our comfort, our Lord, and He rules our lives! I serve Him because His bond is love, His yoke is easy, His burden is light, and His goal for us is abundant life. I follow Him because He's the wisdom of the wise, the power of the powerful, the ancient of days, the ruler of rulers, the leader of all leaders. His goal is a relationship with me. He'll never leave you, never forsake you, never mislead you, never forget you, never overlook you, and never cancel your appointment in His appointment book. When you fall, He'll lift you up. When you fail, He'll forgive you. When you're weak, He's strong. When you're lost, He's your way. When you're afraid, He's your courage. When you stumble, He will steady you. When you're hurt, He's gonna heal you. When you're broken, He will mend you. When you're blind

He will lead you. When you're hungry, He will feed you. When you face trials, He's with you. When I face persecution, He shields me. When I face problems, He will comfort me. When I face loss, He will provide for me. And when we face death, He will carry us all home to meet Him. He is everything, for everybody, everywhere, every time, and in every way. He is your God, and that, Sisters, is who you belong to."

Are you ready to choose faith in your Heavenly Father? Whatever you believe in is what your identity is tied to—you will either use it as a crutch to live the way you want to live, or it will be the reason you live out God's plan in your life.

Are you ready to be who you are meant to be because of who you belong to?

WHO ARE YOU?

Once you grasp the fullness of who you are, it makes you stand a little straighter. It makes you lift your head up a little higher. It gives you new confidence entering a room that God's led you to walk into. It encourages you to pray for those who mock you instead of wanting revenge. It causes you to see ridicule for what it is, which is often a tactic from satan, and helps you resist the urge to be offended by others.

Understanding who you are opens your spiritual eyes and lets you see yourself the way God sees you. It takes the fear out of going where God is leading you, and it opens limitless opportunities to the blessings of your Heavenly Father. It positions you to go where God has called you to go and do those things God has called you to do. So, who are you?

You are a daughter of the King of kings (John 1:12).

You are defined only by Him, and He calls you righteous (2 Corinthians 5:21).

Because you belong to Him, you are blessed and highly favored (Psalm 84:4, AMP).

You are wonderfully and fearfully made (Psalm 139:14).

You are chosen (1 Peter 2:9).

You are forgiven (1 John 1:9).

You are a co-heir with Jesus Christ (Romans 8:17).

You are so precious and important to God that He sent His only Son to be the blood sacrifice so you could choose to live eternally with Him in Heaven (John 3:16).

You are all of the above, but it is up to you to take each of those statements by faith. God's Word becomes evident in your life when you choose to put it to work and believe it. Proverbs 4:23 reminds us that the course of our life depends on what we believe: "Guard your heart above all else, for it determines the course of your life" (NLT). As you gain wisdom and start strengthening your faith in who God is and who He says you are, you will stop countering His view of you with opposing thoughts and statements because your actions will align with His will.

YOUR PURPOSE

How many times have you thought to yourself, "What am I supposed to be doing?" Have you spent a chunk of your life moving from job to job or from career to career trying to find what fulfills you? What if I told you that no specific job or amount of money will ever bring true joy and fulfillment? Sure, you may experience temporary happiness from those things, and money can make things easier, but that is not and should not ever be the focus. Have you ever noticed how many rich people who "have it all" commit suicide? Just in the last decade, we have seen many celebrities end their own lives. Money, fame, and temporary pleasures do not equal contentment and will never replace joy.

You will never experience true freedom and fulfillment without doing what God put you on this earth to do. So why are you here? God created each of us with a purpose. We are here to share Jesus with others and be a blessing to them. Every single one of us was put here to share this message: "For God so loved the world that he gave his one and only Son, that whoever believes in him shall not perish but have eternal life" (John 3:16, NIV). We are to be blessings to others by helping to bring them to salvation and share the love of Jesus (Matthew 28:18-20).

This is your purpose.

ANSWERING THE CALL

YOUR CALLING

Although we are all here for the same purpose, we have each been given a unique calling. Your calling is made up of the gifts, talents, and abilities God created you with, and it's how God wants to partner with you to bring others into His kingdom. There is a need He has equipped you to fulfill. Maybe God has called you to be a teacher, doctor, or social media influencer. He may have called you to be a stay-at-home mom, or maybe you have been gifted a strong business sense or an artistic ability.

1 Peter 4:10 explains, "Each of you should use whatever gift you have received to serve others, as faithful stewards of God's grace in its various forms" (NIV). When God designed you, He designed your life with a special calling, and it's never too late to seek Him for wisdom and direction as to what it is. There are far too many people on Earth who think it is too late, or don't believe they have a specific calling from God. Those who never seek it will miss out on the fulfillment they were meant to experience. James 1:5 states, "If any of you lacks wisdom, you

should ask God, who gives generously to all without finding fault, and it will be given to you" (NIV).

If you have been telling God that one day you will seek Him for your calling, when is that day going to be? Do you understand how important your role is as a part of the body of Christ? If you don't step into what you have been called to, not only are you missing out, but the people you are called to serve are missing out as well. Jesus died for you; when are you going to start living for Him? If you think you don't have time, it's only because you haven't made it a priority. We make time for what we view as important in our lives. Even if you haven't obeyed the call God has instilled in you, it is still there. As long as you are on Earth, God still has a unique plan for your life. That calling and the grace to use it still belong to you. Regardless of how you were raised, your social status, your spiritual walk, your bank account, or anything else, you are still responsible for what you have been called to. Nothing dismisses what God designed you for.

GOD IS CALLING...WILL YOU PICK UP?

God has been calling you. How long have you been hitting the ignore button? Have you struggled to find time for Him in your daily routine? Have you been saying, "I'm too busy," "I'm too tired," or "I'll talk to Him later?" Would you still say those things if He were standing in front of you? If Jesus came over, put His arm around you, and said, "Let's visit," you would respond with the most joyous "Yes!" you have ever given. You would be so overwhelmed with excitement that you would not be able to think about anything else. Nothing would take precedence over that conversation and precious time with Jesus—no other person, no work or appointments, and certainly no TV show.

Why is it different thinking about Jesus standing in front of you than when you feel the tugging at your spirit to spend time with Him? Just because you don't see Him with your natural eyes and don't hear Him with your flesh ears, doesn't mean that He isn't just as real as if He were standing in front of you. We tend to talk to God and treat Him like He is very distant, but He is never out of reach. In 1 Corinthians 6:19, we learn that the Holy Spirit resides within us. This assures us He is never out of reach. Hebrews 13:5 beautifully reinforces this promise with God's words: "I will never leave thee nor forsake thee" (KJV).

Just as you accepted Jesus as your Lord and Savior in faith, you continue developing your relationship with Him through faith. Faith is a knowing that doesn't require seeing to believe. Romans 10:17 tells us faith only comes by hearing the Word of God. We must listen to teachings and the breakdown of scripture so it makes sense to us. That is how we strengthen our faith and put it into action.

The more time you spend with Him, the more knowledge you gain—resulting in stronger faith.

It is time to understand that being a child of God comes with more than just eternity in Heaven. You get the opportunity to have a relationship with your Heavenly Father, and you can choose to say yes to what He has planned and designed you for. Joshua 24:14-15 shares how we have free will to choose whether or not we want to serve Him.

There is never a time when God doesn't provide, but according to the Bible we must do our part. We must have faith in His plans. Everything we need to live a fulfilled life is on the other side of developing our faith in Him so we can say yes to God's plan. Your yes is important to the kingdom of God. There is no fulfillment sweeter than doing what God put you here to do. Whatever calling God has for you, remember it is not about you, it is about the people God can touch through you.

RING. RING. RING.

You: "Hello?"

God: "Hello, Daughter, I have something I need you to do for Me."

You: "Can You tell me more? How much time will it take? Will it take away from my evening TV shows and hanging out with my friends? Will there be a lot required of me? Can You at least fill me in on what steps I will need to take, and while You're at it, what will the result look like? Also, will it cost any money?"

God: "I know you have lots of questions. Do you remember the vision I gave you long ago? The time has come to bring it to life."

You: "But I wouldn't even know where to begin…"

God: "I will give you everything you need to accomplish what I'm asking you to do. All I need from you is to say yes."

You: "I'm embarrassed. What will people think? What will they say? Will people laugh at me?"

God: "None of that matters—the people who need to hear and experience what I'm asking you to do is what matters."

You: "But I've never done anything like this before!"

God: "I have the plan in place. I just need you to say yes."

You: "I am so far from perfect. I don't know how to do what You're asking me to do."

God: "I don't want you to be perfect; no one I have ever used is perfect. You don't need to know how. I will direct each of your steps."

You: "I'm not qualified to do something like this."

God: "Exactly. When I call my children to something, it's for My glory, not theirs. If you were qualified in your own ability, how would other people know it was Me working through you? I will qualify you and equip you with all that you need. You are the only one who can relate to the people I have in mind in the unique way I need it done."

You: "I have a past, and I am still struggling with other things. This is so far beyond my comfort zone."

God: "It's not about you. It's about the people I can touch through you."

You: "But why me?"

God: "I designed you for this before you were born. You are unique and chosen, and I have called you by name for such a time as this. We will do it together."

YOUR ASSIGNMENTS

If our purpose is to glorify God by sharing Him with others through the callings or gifts He has given us, what are we supposed to do? Where do we go, and who do we talk to? I am so grateful we do not have to figure out our own paths. Assignments are tasks we are given to complete using our callings. These assignments are the situations, people, circumstances, and responsibilities God leads us to. Your purpose and calling do not change; however, your assignments often only last for a season in your life.

Did you know you can represent and serve Jesus no matter where you are and what you are doing? As you read more sections in this book, you may find yourself asking, "Where am I called to serve?" You may be thinking, "How do I share Jesus as a stay-at-home mom, or at my corporate job? How do I answer the call on my life?"

You simply do what you know to do that day. God has you where you are right now for a reason. You don't need a big platform to serve where you are, because it is not about the number of followers you have. It is who you follow that means everything. If you are serving God and are obedient to Him, He will lead you where He wants you. No matter what titles you hold, be the hands and feet of Jesus where you are. As a mother, wife, daughter, sister, friend, co-worker, manager, teacher, waitress, or empty nester, you can represent Jesus each day.

When Jesus told the disciples He wouldn't be with them much longer, He said, "'A new command I give you: Love one another. As I have loved you, so you must love one another. By this everyone will know that you are my disciples, if you love one another'" (John 13:34-35, NIV). To share His love is your primary role every day, and that role will lead people into the kingdom of God—even if you don't see it. The example you set for others by being like Jesus is how you are called to represent Him every day.

You know you are supposed to share the unconditional love and unimaginable forgiveness of Jesus with others, but you are curious where to begin. God will give you different assignments to carry out your calling. Maybe God has given you the artistic gift of design, and that is what He has called you to do. You may be assigned to design Bible covers that share messages of faith or clothing that shares scriptures of God's love. When God gives you assignments, He already has the plan and people in mind whose lives you will touch.

When was the last time you were in a situation or crowd wondering what you were doing there? Could it be that God had you there because you were on assignment? Your assignments are how you can use your calling to fulfill God's purpose in your life. He needs us all to do our part to advance His kingdom. Just like a puzzle, if one of us ignores our assignment, there is a piece missing in the body of Christ (1 Corinthians 12:12-27). Staying close to God and remaining in His will is how you develop spiritual ears to hear where the Holy Spirit is leading you.

VISION

YOUR VISION MATTERS

Do you have a vision? Have you ever tried to drive your car in the pouring rain when the windshield wipers were not working? Without your windshield wipers, you cannot see, and you have to pull over—you cannot go anywhere until that rain stops.

Why? Because your vision is impaired. The same thing happens in life. If your vision is impaired, you are not going anywhere. Proverbs 29:18 says, "Where there is no vision, the people cast off restraint; But he that keepeth the law, happy is he" (ASV). "Cast off restraint" emphasizes the significance of God's Word in your life. When you are not following the will of God you are following your own ways, leading to an unfulfilling path that does not bring joy because it is outside of His plan.

You must have a vision, and you must surround yourself with what can be and not just what is. Your vision is connected to your calling. What are the dreams and goals you want to accomplish? If you don't have any, you have no vision and nothing will happen. It's as simple as this: If you expect nothing, you will have nothing. Set aside time to focus on your vision. Has God revealed something to you in the past? When you think about your future, do you have desires that have always been there? Those desires may be there because God is giving you a vision for your future.

UNDERSTAND YOUR VISION

Vision is: "the ability to think about or plan the future with imagination or wisdom" (Oxford Languages). I want you to remember these two words: imagination and wisdom. Using your imagination is a true gift when it comes to having a vision, and it is available to all. Being able to imagine is to see things differently than they are right now. Without imagination, you will stay in the same place and continue doing the same things.

Consider what Proverbs 2:6 tells us: "For the Lord gives wisdom; from his mouth come knowledge and understanding" (NIV). Because vision consists of both imagination and wisdom, having an imagination without wisdom would result in not being able to see the fullness of your vision. To experience full vision in your life, you must seek wisdom from the only place you can gain true wisdom: God.

Maybe you know God has real insight, but you are unsure how to obtain it from Him. Don't worry; instead, turn to scripture and it will explain in detail what you should do. "If any of you lacks wisdom, you should ask God, who gives generously to all without finding fault, and it will be given to you. But when you ask, you must believe and not doubt, because the one who doubts is like a wave of the sea, blown and tossed by the wind" (James 1:5-6, NIV).

When you seek God for wisdom, you must ask in full expectation that you will receive wisdom from Him. Keeping the Word in front of your eyes and in your ears will fill you up with truth, which continually pushes doubt out.

CLARIFY YOUR VISION

God gives specific instructions about how to handle your vision. Proverbs 29:18 reminds us that we must first have a vision, and that it is life-giving. He also instructs us to, "...Write the vision; make it plain..." (Habakkuk 2:2, ESV). When something is made plain, it doesn't cause confusion. Your vision should be specific so it will be clear.

When you think about your family, what is your vision? Do you think in general terms of only wanting them to be happy and healthy, or do you have specific things you want for them, such as happy marriages, and guidance in making the right decisions? How about your finances? Would you like to see an increase in both your income and debt cancellation this year? Do you know how much you need in order to be debt-free? If you are asking God to help you with debt freedom, are you asking Him for a specific amount? He doesn't give you what you don't ask for because you don't have the faith to receive it. If you ask God for an increase, don't be surprised if it's an extra $50 this year.

Being specific isn't just for you, it's for God too. He wouldn't tell you to be specific if He didn't want you to be specific. When it comes to your vision, how clear are you on it? Is the vision clear enough to write down? If not, heed the instruction from James 1:5-6: Seek Him and believe you will receive. When you are clear, write your vision down plainly.

FELLOWSHIP WITH YOUR VISION

First, you must spend time with God getting wisdom on what the vision is. Then, you must write down clearly and specifically what God tells you. This is not where the instruction for visions ends. Proverbs 23:7 explains that whatever your heart is rooted in is who you will become. What is in your heart matters and holds the key to your future.

So how do you control what is in your heart? It is very simple: You decide what you focus on. Keep the vision before your eyes so you can achieve your dreams. With the chaos and never-ending distractions from day-to-day life, people forget what their vision is. With each day that you don't focus on your vision, its value becomes less in your heart. What you think about, you bring about. Fellowshipping with your vision requires you to have it in your thoughts constantly. God will give you creative ideas to bring that vision to life.

I once heard about a woman diagnosed with terminal cancer. When she looked in the mirror, all she saw was death. Because she no longer looked healthy and lively, she couldn't see herself as healed, and she continually thought about how different she looked now compared to months before. She knew she didn't have much time, and she was praying for healing while standing in faith on healing scriptures, but then she remembered James 2:26: "...faith without works is dead..." (NKJV). Faith is believing in what you cannot see. This woman needed to believe the unseen and to use her imagination by keeping the vision before her eyes. She needed to see herself as healed.

She put her faith into action by printing pictures of herself before she was diagnosed with terminal cancer and taping them all over her bathroom mirror so that is the only vision she would see. She started to see herself lively and healed like she once was. Miraculously, this woman was told at one of her subsequent appointments that the cancer was gone! Isn't that amazing?

This is the power of vision. You must start seeing things differently than what they are at this moment. You will never believe you can accomplish your big dreams if you don't get clear on your vision, write it down, and keep it before your eyes, refusing to allow the present to take away from the future God wants for you.

REPRESENTING JESUS

CALLED TO LOVE

What does it look like to represent Jesus? Representing Jesus is not about trying to be Superwoman and doing everything you see others doing. Representing Jesus is quite simple—although it's not always easy.

Representing Jesus means to be like Jesus. How can you be His hands and feet today, even if you are unsure of what your calling is? To represent His love, you must live from a place of love. Ephesians 5:1-2 paints a picture of how we are to represent Jesus, and Paul explains we are to "Follow God's example, therefore, as dearly loved children and walk in the way of love, just as Christ loved us and gave himself up for us as a fragrant offering and sacrifice to God" (NIV). You cannot thoroughly share Jesus with others if you are not walking in love.

Ephesians 4 tells us to walk in unity, reminds us we are no longer who we were before becoming a Christian, and shares that we are equipped and given the grace to do what God has called us to do. Paul even tells us what not to do, which allows us to represent Jesus to the fullest.

As you press into walking boldly and completely in the calling of God in your life, you must walk in love and forgiveness. Proof of what is in your heart comes from the words you speak, and the Bible tells us in Luke 6:45, "...for out of the abundance of the heart his mouth speaks..." (ESV). If you want to fully and confidently represent God, get aligned with His Word so it flows from your mouth.

How well would we represent Jesus if we became even half as determined as Paul was to know Him? In Philippians 3:12, he says, "Not that I have already obtained all this, or have already arrived at my goal, but I press on to take hold of that for which Christ Jesus took hold of me" (NIV). Paul is in active pursuit of Jesus, and this is the attitude we should all take on. We should be pressing into God and His Word until we get to Heaven and hear "...Well done, good and faithful servant!..." (Matthew 25:21, NIV). That heart cry to know God kept Paul focused on bringing more people to God's kingdom each day because he was committed to fulfilling the calling of God in his life. Laying down our desires so we can be in alignment with our Father and saying yes wholeheartedly is what will push us toward the goal of truly knowing Jesus and sharing Him boldly.

Knowing Him intimately creates an excitement for life and an eagerness to share Him so others can choose to spend eternity with Him. It is a pure joy and excitement bursting from the seams of your being. It creates an inner glow that is reflected to others. Have you ever looked at someone and seen

Jesus's glow shining through them? Those people have spent a lot of throne time with God. They desire Him so much that they become full of Him, and that is the glow you can literally see shining through them.

Haven't we all been called to be like Him? But how can we be like Him if we are not spending that quality time with Him? We can't. We must know Him to be like Him in order to represent Him. We need to spend that precious time getting to know Him, which is far different than knowing of Him. The more you know Him, the more you want to share Him. The more work He does in you, the more you can't help but share Him with others because your heart becomes full of Him, His joy, and His love.

DON'T NEGATE THE SMALLER THINGS

Have you ever been given an everyday task that you felt was beneath you? Maybe your boss asked you to do something that you handed off to a coworker, or your friend needed help with something that you said no to even though you had the time and resources. Has God ever given you a task that you ignored because you thought it wasn't a big deal? God always gives us smaller tasks before He gives us the bigger ones, and this is how many of us learn to be obedient. He must be able to trust you will do the right thing. "Whoever can be trusted with very little can also be trusted with much, and whoever is dishonest with very little will also be dishonest with much" (Luke 16:10, NIV).

The book of 1 Samuel shares how Saul became king. Do you know that it was an act of obedience that put Saul in the position to become king? He was looking for his father's animals. He could have passed the job along to someone else; there were plenty of others who could have done it. Because Saul said yes to his father, the meeting between Saul and Samuel took place, and it was this meeting which ultimately led to him becoming king.

What have you missed out on because you said no to things you didn't feel like doing or to tasks that didn't seem important to you? Even as I write these words, I am asking myself the same question. What a great reminder to ask God to order our steps each day. After all, Psalm 37:23 tells us, "The steps of a good man are ordered by the Lord, And He delights in his way" (NKJV).

Some days our routine household tasks are exhausting. We do the laundry, make the meals, prepare the lunches, go to the grocery store, clean the house, sweep the floors, feed the dogs, water the plants, and the list goes on. I know I am not the only one who has wondered if anyone appreciates all I do, or the only one who has questioned why we do all these unnoticed things. Then I am reminded of Rebekah's story in the book of Genesis.

One day while Rebekah was doing one of her

own everyday tasks—fetching water from the well—she met one of Abraham's servants who was praying God would lead Him to the woman he was supposed to bring to marry Isaac. I have wondered how many times Rebekah walked to and from that well fetching water. She didn't say, "No one appreciates what I do, so why do I even bother?" She just did what she knew to do that day, which ultimately resulted in fulfilled prophecies.

Not all tasks are going to set you up for royalty or lead you to your husband as Saul and Rebecca experienced. However, when you are obedient to the Lord's leading, His favor is upon you. Your obedience allows Him to do more in your life. The Word reminds us in Deuteronomy 28:2, "And all these blessings shall come upon you and overtake you, if you obey the voice of the Lord your God" (ESV).

HOW DO I HEAR FROM GOD?

POSITION YOURSELF

To partner with God on His assignments for you, you must be in the right position, or you will allow anything to distract you from His direction. Almost everything in life requires correct positioning, and it is an important key to becoming successful at anything—graduating college, saving money for a down payment on your dream home, even building a strong foundation for your marriage. Positioning yourself well means preparing and choosing to stay focused.

Hearing from God is no different. Many Christians seem to think that hearing from God means begging and struggling for answers. Rather, it's about being expectant, consistent, and obedient with the time you spend with Him. When you focus on these three things, you are learning to seek Him and His kingdom above everything else, which is what Jesus commands us to do in Matthew 6:33. When you choose to make God your number one priority, you are putting yourself in a position to hear from Him. As you learn His ways, you are strengthening your faith and learning how to trust and receive what He has for you.

Expect to hear from God. The person who doesn't expect to hear God will not, and if you are not expectant, you will make yourself believe it was just a coincidence when you do hear from Him. You must be full of expectation. How do you stay in full expectation? You stay close to Him. Jesus reminds us in John 15:4, "Remain in me, as I also remain in you. No branch can bear fruit by itself; it must re-main in the vine. Neither can you bear fruit unless you remain in me" (NIV). To abide means to stay or remain. If you stop abiding in Him, you will abide in something of this world instead. What you abide in is where your focus is. Repeat this daily, "I am His sheep, and I hear Him" (John 10:14).

Position yourself in the flow of faith. Life is not perfect, and you will face opposition from the enemy as you start spending more time with God. Because his main agenda is to steal the Word of God from you, satan will undoubtedly do his best to distract you from your relationship with your Father. The distractions often come in the form of inconve-niences such as a flat tire, sickness, or an unexpect-ant financial burden. In James 4:7 we are told how to handle opposition: "Submit yourselves, then, to God. Resist the devil, and he will flee from you" (NIV). As your faith grows, resisting satan becomes easier because you are positioned well.

Hearing from God does not have to be a struggle. Make sure you are positioned well by abiding in His Word so your expectancy is in Him and in hearing from Him. According to Psalm 32:8, God uses His Word to direct, guide, and command you: "I will instruct you and teach you in the way you should go; I will counsel you with my loving eye on you" (NIV).

DEVELOP EARS TO HEAR

If you've read *The Covenant Woman*, then you already know I struggled to hear from God when I began asking Him about my calling. My issue wasn't just that I didn't allow God any room to speak—my bigger mistake was that I wasn't following His direction for my life. While I was seeking and begging God for answers, I was not obeying Him in a separate situation He gave me clear direction on. He needed me to surrender a relationship that was causing me to view myself as less than He views me. Because I was tying my identity to how the relationship made me feel, it was hindering what He could do through me. God knew I would have never said yes to the assignments He has for me while I looked to a relationship outside of Him to be my source of joy and fulfillment.

To hear from God, you need to be purposeful in staying on His path for your life. If you are unwilling or just flat out ignorant of His will, He knows you aren't going to be obedient when it comes to His direction. If you refuse to spend time with Him and in growing your knowledge in His Word, how will you know what you are supposed to do? If you don't develop the ears to hear, how will you hear His call? Jeremiah 29:11 shares how His plans are indeed good and that He cares about your future, but it takes faith to believe those things are true. Scripture teaches, "... faith comes by hearing, and hearing by the word of God" (Romans 10:17, NKJV).

You've been wondering what your calling is for quite some time now. Have you asked everyone except for the One who has the answer? Seeing others live out the call of God in their lives may cause you to think they can guide you to your calling, but it is important to remember they don't have your answers. Sure, they have wisdom and can give you words of encouragement and possibly some guidance, but do not put more time and faith into a person than you do God.

Even when it feels like He is not hearing you, He is the One with your answers. If you are not hearing Him, ask yourself if you have ears to hear. I am not referring to physical ears on the side of your head. I am referring to the spiritual ears Jesus talks about in Mark 4:9: "Then Jesus said, 'Whoever has ears to hear, let them hear'" (NIV). He is sharing the parable of the sower and the seed, and explains that all people can hear His Word, but only some will be fruitful with it. If your relationship with Him is not made the main priority in your life, you will allow anything to take away what He gives you or shares with you, including wisdom and guidance. Do you have the spiritual ears to hear Him and heed the Holy Spirit's direction?

SEEKING GOD FOR YOUR UNIQUE CALLING

PARTNERING WITH GOD

When God puts a calling in your heart, He wants to be in partnership with you. Take a moment to consider that. Your Heavenly Father wants you to partner up with Him. This is why it is so important that you are fellowshipping with His vision and aligning your will and desire with His.

The key to partnering with God will always be to follow the command in Matthew 6:33, which perfectly illustrates how to live out God's plan for your life: "But seek first his kingdom and his righteousness, and all these things will be given to you as well" (NIV). I refer to this scripture as the key to life because it tells us how to live. When you choose to keep this command, you choose to keep the rest of His commands because you are seeking His way of doing everything. Seeking God above all things allows His will to be done in every area of your life.

What does it look like to truly seek God's way of doing things? It is action. It is the act of learning what the Word of God says and obeying it. To know the Word is to know Him. What He says has always been, is now, and will always be 100% true. Nothing trumps His Word—not a fact, not what your natural eyes can see, not your feelings, and not the opinions of another person. Come to God through His Word. This is how you get to know Him. You learn of His love for you, His forgiveness for you, and His favor on you through learning who He is and how He does things. From knowledge comes faith, and from faith comes action.

In addition to studying and learning the Word of God, you also can get to know Him through spending time in prayer and fellowship with Him. Just like building any other relationship in your life, spending time together strengthens your relationship with Him. The Word of God is how you learn His will and way of doing things. Fellowshipping with Him is how you get step-by-step directions and guidance.

RECOGNIZING YOUR CALLING

Your calling and the assignments God has for you are between you and Him. No other person can tell you what God has called you to do, and that includes me. I can, however, provide assurance on things to remember as you are pressing into Him and seeking His guidance on your calling.

The calling God has designed for you will never contradict scripture. 2 Timothy 3:16-17 shares, "All Scripture is God-breathed and is useful for teaching, rebuking, correcting and training in righteousness, so that the servant of God may be thoroughly equipped for every good work" (NIV). If you feel led or pulled to do something that goes against scripture, this is evidence it is not from God.

Although your assignments will often feel out of your comfort zone, they come with the peace of God, and He doesn't live in overwhelm. Think of His character traits, the fruit of the Spirit. We find that list in Galatians 5:22-23, "love, joy, peace, patience, kindness, goodness, faithfulness, gentleness, and self-control" (NLT). Jesus is even called the "Prince of Peace" in Isaiah 9:6. The peace of God is talked about throughout the Bible. We know He doesn't want us to be overwhelmed and overworked because those feelings contradict His peace.

Always remember that your calling will point people to Jesus and glorify Him in the process. God will never call you into anything that doesn't bring Him glory. Peter urges Christians to be like Jesus and to remember that serving Him is not for our own glory in 1 Peter 4:10-11:

Each of you should use whatever gift you have received to serve others, as faithful stewards of God's grace in its various forms. If anyone speaks, they should do so as one who speaks the very words of God. If anyone serves, they should do so with the strength God provides, so that in all things God may be praised through Jesus Christ. To him be the glory and the power for ever and ever. Amen (NIV).

ALLOW GOD TO EQUIP YOU

The reason people get nervous when God calls them to do something is that initial feeling of having to accomplish it through their own abilities. For me, I couldn't even figure out step number one of the assignments He gave me without His guidance and grace, and I am so thankful I didn't have to. If you could do it on your own, it wouldn't be a calling from God. Do not try to equip yourself, and certainly do not allow the world to equip you. When we start trying to self-equip, we make wrong decisions and are influenced by the wrong things—worldly things.

Paul reminds us that if God calls us to a task, He will also give us what we need to accomplish it: "I thank Christ Jesus our Lord, who has given me strength, that he considered me trustworthy, appointing me to his service" (1 Timothy 1:12, NIV). It is our Heavenly Father who makes us able; therefore, we do not rest in our own ability, we believe in His Word and rely on His guidance. Because God handles the preparation, you must trust that the provision for each assignment has already been met. He has already taken care of the arrangements, which means the supply level is full, including any resources needed to carry out every assignment.

ONE STEP AT A TIME

We are all about the big picture, aren't we? We want to know who, what, where, when, and why. We are curious beings. I have found that "When?" and "How?" are usually the questions people want answered before saying yes to God's assignments. Before taking on an assignment from God, we innately want to know what our friends will think, how much judgment we will get, and how much of a sacrifice we will need to make. Maybe that's why God doesn't show us the big picture: He wants our obedience no matter the sacrifices required.

Our obedience shows our love and faithfulness to Him. He never tells us to do anything we are incapable of doing when we lean on His guidance and power. We know we can trust God, and we have experienced His love for us. He has never lied to us and has always remained faithful to His Word. He doesn't overwhelm you by showing you the end result or the minutiae of how to get there.

In John 15:16, Jesus said, "You did not choose me, but I chose you and appointed you so that you might go and bear fruit—fruit that will last—and so that whatever you ask in my name the Father will give you" (NIV). God designed each assignment to bring forth fruit, so He gives you one step at a time. Just like the fruit we eat, our faith starts out as a seed. When that tiny seed grows in the right environment, it becomes what it was created to be. Jesus explains in John 15:4 that the fruit comes from abiding in Him. When we stay close to Him, we want to be in His will. The fruit Jesus is referring to is our living in His blessings and sharing them with others. As we abide in Him, we bring forth fruit, and then God gives us what we ask in the name of Jesus (John 15:4-16, NKJV). These answered prayers become testimonies that lead others to Him.

Can you imagine what would go through your mind if God gave you fifty tasks to accomplish at once? It wouldn't matter if they were all small; you would feel overwhelmed, and when you are overwhelmed you most likely freeze. You would end up taking no action because you would be unsure of how and where to start. Think about the last time you deep-cleaned something. Did you start by taking everything out of what you were cleaning? Then did you stand and stare at it—wondering where to start—while questioning why you started this project in the first place?

If you're anything like me, you begin with one pile of things, and five minutes later you're going through a box of pictures for the next half hour. Now you have a bigger mess than you started with, but you probably continued to distractedly jump from one task to another, hoping to see some type of progress. It is overwhelming, isn't it? If God gave you all the steps of your assignment at one time, you would get distracted and overwhelmed, thinking, "This is too much!"

He is so gracious, and He wants to make sure you are prepared. He has no intention of throwing it at you all at once. It's like when you are teaching a baby how to eat. You don't hand her a knife and fork; you give her a spoon. Then you show her how to dip the spoon into the mashed carrots. Finally, you show her how to put it in her mouth.

It is messy, isn't it? Do you scream at your baby and tell her how big of a mess she is making? Of course not! You tell her how amazing she is and what a great job she is doing. This is how God gives you the steps for your assignments. He is watching you, and He is proud of you. He takes pleasure in your obedience, and He says, "...My grace is sufficient for you, for my power is made perfect in weakness..." (2 Corinthians 12:9, NIV). He just needs your willing, obedient heart to do what He is asking you to do. He is not expecting perfection—perfection is not in God's plan for you. If you were perfect, you wouldn't need His grace.

DON'T ALLOW OPPOSITION TO OVERPOWER THE CALL

BLOCK OUT THE NOISE

Many distractions keep us from spending time with God even when we feel His leading to do so. Humanity has become ridiculously busy being focused on this thing or that. This world is a distracting place, isn't it? The Bible says satan is the god of this world (2 Corinthians 4:4, NLT). Stealing the Word of God from you and distracting you from your relationship with your Heavenly Father is his biggest agenda. It's not just distractions that keep us from spending time with God. We also seem to ignore or shy away from Him when we feel overwhelmed, confused, not good enough, ashamed, lost, or unfulfilled. Each of these feelings comes from satan and/or not spending the quality time with God that our spirits hunger for.

Has satan tried to tell you that you are too late to fulfill God's plan? Has he made you believe you have wasted too much time? Do you remember how long Jesus's earthly ministry was? Three years. The ministry that saved the world was accomplished in three years. There is a ton that can be packed into a small amount of time. Don't let the enemy tell you that you wasted too much of your life and have no time left. Remember, that is just a strategy of satan. God needs you to know that He is your fulfillment. He has the answer to your every prayer. The hope you thought was gone; He wants to restore it. Any shame you're carrying around, the loneliness you have been engulfed in, that lost feeling you may have: it all can only be changed by the presence of God. When you follow His direction, you allow Him to order your steps and His blessings to overtake you.

RENEW YOUR MIND

When you say yes to God's call on your life, opposition will come from every side, which is why you must have a firm grasp on Him, His Word, and what He has called you to. When you are firmly planted in God's instruction, it will not matter what the devil throws at you, and it bears no weight when you know who you are in Christ.

When you are partnering with God on His plan for your life, you must stay focused on the assignment. If you find yourself constantly weighed down and battling opposition, know this is not in His plan. One of the most beautiful things about living in God's plan is that you don't have to be in constant battle—He battles for you. Your responsibility is to continually renew your mind. If you do not have a renewed mind, you will lose focus and allow every strategy from the enemy to wear you down. An unrenewed mind is exhausted because it is full of what the opposition says, and it is a mind full of burdens.

How do you renew your mind? You must replace any thoughts you have that aren't of God with His thoughts. To have a renewed mind, you must be in the presence of God consistently and fill yourself with His Word. Our future is based on that which fills our mind, and opposition cannot survive against the truth. Romans 12:2 states, "Do not conform to the pattern of this world, but be transformed by the renewing of your mind. Then you will be able to test and approve what God's will is—his good, pleasing and perfect will" (NIV).

When you have an opposing thought such as: "I can't do this," You must tell yourself, "It's a good thing I don't have to do it on my own. According to Philippians 2:13, it is God in me accomplishing it. Praise the Lord!" Scripture even tells us to bring God into every accusation and every argumentative thought that is combative against His Word. "We destroy arguments and every lofty opinion raised against the knowledge of God, and take every thought captive to obey Christ" (2 Corinthian 10:5, ESV). You cannot allow opposing thoughts to become words you speak and therefore believe. You must renew your mind in God's Word, and let

His Word be the flow of your life. Philippians 4:8 instructs us, "Finally, brethren, whatever things are true, whatever things are noble, whatever things are just, whatever things are pure, whatever things are lovely, whatever things are of good report, if there is any virtue, and if there is anything praiseworthy—meditate on these things" (NKJV).

RELEASE GUILT AND SHAME

I receive dozens of emails, messages, and comments weekly from women telling me how they feel God tugging at their hearts to do something for His kingdom, but they don't feel good enough because of the shame and guilt they carry from their past. If you feel the same way, I want you to know that you are not alone. But know this: God loves you so much, and just like His love for you is unchanging, His plans for you are also unchanging. He already knows exactly what will happen throughout your life, and He knows every decision you will ever make—good or bad.

Burn these words into your heart and never forget them: God is not mad at you. Your past only enhances what God can do for you, through you, and with you in your future. Although it's hard to believe that when you are in the throes of a hard situation, remember that He can use every season for His good and His glory (Romans 8:28). Have you ever noticed that most of the people you follow, look up to, or are inspired by, all have a story that started with a difficult season of grief, loneliness, anger, or sickness before they experienced victory? They are relatable because of what they've walked through. God uses our pasts as testimonies to help others.

When Jesus died on the cross, He took on every ounce of shame and guilt for everyone, including you. He didn't do it for fun; He did it so you wouldn't have to carry the burden and pain of shame. He doesn't want that for you. When you are buried in shame, it feels like a heavy weight you cannot get out from under. Some people are sad when they are buried in shame, others try to mask it with anger. When you are surrounded by shame, you don't think much of yourself, you have no peace or joy, you feel unworthy, unwanted, unnecessary, and defeated. Your thought life is a wreck when you think you are not good enough, and your words will always align with your thoughts, so of course you speak negative things over and about yourself. You end up lashing out at people you love, get offended very easily, and would rather stay in bed than be productive, because it feels like nothing matters.

Do you think those feelings come from God or satan? The Bible clearly explains the difference between what God wants for you and what the enemy wants for you. Jesus said, "The thief comes only to steal and kill and destroy; I have come that they may have life, and have it to the full" (John 10:10, NIV). God says you're righteous (2 Corinthians 5:21). He knew every mistake you would make, and still wants you to spend eternity with Him (Romans 8:38-39).

He loves you so much that He sent Jesus to die for your shame, among other things (1 John 4:9-10). When you are in a shame funk, what is the number one thing you don't want to do? You do not want to talk to God or be in the Word. satan wants you to feel so ashamed that you turn away from God, feeling unworthy to talk to the only one who gives you peace. He wants to keep you distracted because he knows God is the only one who can take the shame and pain away. If he can get you into a shame spiral, he is doing his job well.

Living in shame is barely living at all, making you feel and act like someone you were never meant to be. That is not God's design for your life. How do you break free from the shame and guilt of your past? Whether it was something you did or something that was done to you, you must decide to believe what God says about you and not the enemy's lies. Ask God for forgiveness, "'I, even I, am he who blots out your transgressions, for my own sake, and remembers your sins no more'" (Isaiah 43:25, NIV). Jesus paid the price for your sin (Isaiah 53:5), took on the burden of shame (Hebrews 12:2), and traded them for His righteousness (2 Corinthians 5:21).

EMBRACE YOUR GREATNESS

2 Corinthians 5:7 reminds us, "For we walk by faith, not by sight" (NKJV). God must have known we would be tempted to focus on what we could see rather than what His Word says. When we walk by sight, we negate the power and anointing in God's plan. If you choose to always live by what you see, you will never fulfill God's plan for your life.

This reminds me of the Isrealites who watched God perform miracle after miracle. He told the people He had land awaiting them, and in Exodus 3:17, describes it as "...a land flowing with milk and honey" (KJV). He was ready to make the land theirs, but He still needed the Israelites' obedience in order to work through them.

You may say to yourselves, 'These nations are stronger than we are. How can we drive them out?' But do not be afraid of them; remember well what the Lord your God did to Pharaoh and to all Egypt. You saw with your own eyes the great trials, the signs and wonders, the mighty hand and outstretched arm, with which the Lord your God brought you out. The Lord your God will do the same to all the peoples you now fear. Moreover, the Lord your God will send the hornet among them until even the survivors who hide from you have perished. Do not be terrified by them, for the Lord your God, who is among you, is a great and awesome God (Deuteronomy 7:17-21, NIV).

When Moses sent twelve men to check out the land, they reported, "We went into the land to which you sent us, and it does flow with milk and honey! Here is its fruit. But the people who live there are powerful, and the cities are fortified and very large..." (Numbers 13:27-28, NIV). In verse thirty-one we can see their mindset as they said, "...We can't attack those people; they are stronger than we are." The disobedience and thoughts of these people resulted in only two men from that generation entering the Promised Land. All of the others missed out because they focused on what they could see, and not their faith in the power of God. Because they did not trust God, the Isrealites didn't take the steps He told them to take, and Caleb and Joshua were the only ones who chose not to be moved by what they saw, and continued to believe what God said regardless of the giants in front of them. Their faith was pleasing to God, and He rewarded them by allowing them to enter the Promised Land.

Like many Christians today, the Isrealites decided to focus on their own ability instead of God's power, even after seeing the miracles He had performed. I believe we have all seen miracles in our lives, yet we still allow what we can see to hinder the call from God. God has the entire plan orchestrated. Do not allow the giants in front of you to make you forget the greatness of the One who lives within you. The greater one, God, is more powerful than any giant or obstacle you will ever face, and He has the supply you need to face anything. He is the laborer; you are the co-laborer. As you stay in the flow of renewing your mind to His Word, you will not flee from opposition like the Isrealites did.

STAY IN YOUR LANE

KEEP THE MAIN THING THE MAIN THING

To succeed in completing your assignments, you must make it a priority. It's important to have clarity about where God told you to go and what He told you to do. If you're like most busy adults in this world, your brain can feel like it is firing on all cylinders, all the time. Do you ever feel like the to-do lists are never-ending? Being there for your spouse, raising your children, paying bills, cleaning the house, keeping up with yard work, trying to be a good friend, checking in with your loved ones, making nutritious meals, doing the laundry, being a good employee, attending school functions, answering important emails, making and getting everyone to their appointments, and trying to stay physically healthy can feel very chaotic. This is why it is crucial to be in constant fellowship with God. He knows everything you have on your plate, so He knows how to guide you through each step of what He is asking you to do, which is another reason God only gives you one step at a time.

When we are trying to focus on too many things at once, we forget where our focus should be. If God has already given you an assignment, ask yourself if you are staying focused on each step. The world will shove dozens of extra things in front of you daily. For example, if God told you to write a book, your mind may now be overloaded from thinking about creating a website, marketing your book, designing the cover, sharing information on social media, and so on... Are all those things important? Absolutely. There is a time to focus on each of those tasks. Should they take the place of the main thing God told you to focus on? Absolutely not. Set aside specific time to work on those things, but do not let them take precedence over the first step God told you to take. No matter what your assignment is, your number one priority is to always seek Him and His way of doing things above everything else.

STOP SAYING YES TO EVERYTHING

Until a few years ago, whenever someone would ask me for something, I would drop whatever important thing I was working on to please someone else. It made my stomach hurt to think I upset someone or couldn't help them. I am the person in my family who doesn't mind a challenge and knows everything is figure-outable, which also means I have enabled many people in my life. Maybe this describes you as well. Perhaps you constantly drop what you are working on to help others.

If we are focused on pleasing people constantly, we are choosing to say yes to things God never told us to say yes to and saying no to God. How often have you thought, "I don't have time to read my Bible today," or said, "God, I don't have time to get direction on where you want to lead me today. I will try to make time for you tomorrow, but tonight I'm just too tired." Even if you've never said these words, what do your actions say? If you are saying yes to everyone else, and then you turn around and say no to God, it hinders the work He wants to do through you.

Remember when you say yes to God, you cannot say yes to everyone and everything else. No one person can do it all. You can't say yes to every phone call, every lunch date, every interview, or even every time you're asked to volunteer at your kid's school. It's not greedy to stay focused on God's assignment for you or where He is leading you. It is pleasing to Him, and that is where our focus should be. In Galatians 1:10, Paul warns: "If I were still trying to please people, I would not be a servant of Christ" (NIV).

While working on my own assignments from God, I have had days where I have been overwhelmed from saying yes to others instead of politely saying, "I do not have the extra time to do that." There are things I'm still learning to delegate. My advice? Weekly (or daily) designate time for the assignment you are working on, and do not allow anything to distract you from it. Let your family know you are working on something, delegate where you can, and turn your phone on Do Not Disturb. These are the most helpful things I have done while working on the assignments God has given me.

TAKING ON UNASSIGNED TASKS

As a woman of faith, I love sharing how good our God is, and I am drawn to anything related to faith: messages, writings, songs, clothing, etc. Because I am drawn to it, it feels so natural to simply say yes. I am still learning to ask myself, "Did God tell me to do this?"

Weekly, I get hundreds of messages and emails asking me to promote products in exchange for a commission on TikTok because I have a platform with tens of thousands of followers. It would be easy to say yes to faith-based products, but God has made it clear to me that is not what He wants me to do. Could that change? It's possible, but I'm okay if it never does. I enjoy being where He has called me to be while doing what He has called me to do, and I have not been called to do all things.

For example, I share my love for Jesus and His love for you, but I am not a preacher, counselor, or someone who knows everything about the path you should take. I am learning to stay in my lane and give myself permission to not take on what God has not assigned to me, and it has been one of the best things I have done for myself. Saying yes to God will require you to say no to other people and opportunities, but being in alignment with God's direction brings more peace.

Think of all the tasks you say yes to that God didn't tell you to engage in. Of course you feel worn out. He didn't tell you to take on those extra responsibilities. When you don't feel fulfilled, it tends to make you feel unsettled, like something is lacking. A sure way to get off course from where God told you to be is to start trying to fulfill yourself. This takes a toll on you mentally, spiritually, and physically. If you don't feel fulfilled, then you allow this world to fulfill you. On the days you feel a lack of fulfillment, remember the cure is time with Jesus, as it says in Matthew 11:28-30: "'Come to me, all you who are weary and burdened, and I will give you rest. Take my yoke upon you and learn from me, for I am gentle and humble in heart, and you will find rest for your souls. For my yoke is easy and my burden is light'" (NIV).

You won't always understand why He tells you to do some things and not others, but you don't have to understand in order to obey Him. What you need to understand is that He always has your best interest at heart. "'For my thoughts are not your thoughts, neither are your ways my ways,' declares the Lord. 'As the heavens are higher than the earth, so are my ways higher than your ways and my thoughts than your thoughts'" (Isaiah 55:8-9, NIV). God needs you to stick to the plan He has for you. Taking on tasks He has not assigned you will lead to overwhelm and distraction, causing you to miss out on fulfillment and not bring His plan for your life to completion.

STOP ASKING FOR DIRECTIONS FROM THOSE WHO HAVE NEVER BEEN WHERE YOU ARE GOING

SEEK HIM, NOT THEM

When you are going on a trip or to an unfamiliar place, whom do you call for directions? Do you call your mom who doesn't like leaving her house? Do you ask your best friend who never leaves the small town she lives in? Why in the world would you ask someone for directions to a place they have never been? It is like asking a dentist a question you should be asking a lawyer. When it comes to the assignments God puts in your heart, why would you ask another person for their opinion?

God doesn't tell everyone else what He wants you to do. It is critical you understand this so you stop seeking others' permission, validation, and approval to do what God is telling you to do and go where God is leading you. Do you want to feel like you heard God wrong? Do you want to feel defeated, unworthy, and unqualified? When you ask someone who is not on the same path what they think about your big dreams, desires, and visions, that is what usually happens. It's the quickest way to shut down and believe you cannot accomplish what God designed you for.

God is not talking to others about your calling and assignments, which is why it is so important to be grounded in what the Lord has put on your heart. Other people don't understand, and they will inevitably discourage you even if it's not on purpose. They will automatically start speaking from a lack of qualification. People do this because they aren't equipped for what God has called you for. They may tell you about a bad experience or someone else's failure, though it isn't always done to discourage you. More often than not, these types of conversations are a result of the love the person has for you. In their minds, they are looking out for you, and they don't want you to fail. However, God is giving the assignment to you, He doesn't need them to bless, approve, or even agree with it. When God told Noah to build the ark, what would have happened if he listened to those that mocked him and called him a fool?

It is vital to ask God who you can share your assignments with. Sometimes, He doesn't want you talking to anyone about it for a long time, and other times, He will give you specific people to talk to because you need the knowledge they have. Your assignments are precious to the kingdom and must be handled delicately. Protect and honor what God gives you, and let Him lead you to those you can discuss it with.

THEY DON'T KNOW WHAT THEY DON'T KNOW

Understanding that others are not on the same path as you will help you tremendously. In September of 2021, as I was waiting to board a plane at the Oklahoma City airport, I logged into my email to see that the contract I had discussed with my publishing agent for *The Covenant Woman* was ready to be signed. I quickly read it over and signed before I had to board. I had begun to let fear turn into excitement as I was looking forward to sharing God's message with others.

Later that evening, I met up with some friends for dinner and was eager to share what I had partnered up with God on. As I was sharing some of the details, one of them looked me straight in the eye and said, "Do not name your book *The Covenant Woman.*" I was immediately confused, and I remember saying, "But God told me to." My friend went further, saying, "God told you in a way that you would understand what He was saying, but I've written books with faith titles, and it just doesn't work. You can still have the same content, but do not title your book *The Covenant Woman.*"

It hurt my feelings at first, but then I started wondering if that person was right. God spoke to my heart right then, saying, "I gave you this assignment, not them." I knew I heard from God, and I didn't need this person or any other person to agree with the title for it to be what God wanted it to be. Was my friend trying to hurt me or discourage me? No. They were basing their opinion on their experience, so why would I allow that to discourage me from what I know God told me to do? I am so grateful I chose to obey what I heard God say to me. In fact, since the book was published, several women have told me they purchased the book purely because the title spoke to them.

Just like God works through us, satan works through people too, and he is the author of confusion. satan was trying to confuse me about the title of my book. Had I chosen to be disobedient in the title of the book, it would have prevented some women from reading it. God has every detail for each assignment planned out. Don't allow the enemy to confuse you on what you know God told you.

WHY IS GOD MAKING ME WAIT?

HE IS THE GIVER, NOT THE WITHHOLDER

It is time to stop wasting another second of your life wondering why God's timing is not the same as yours. Even though His timing often doesn't make sense to us, it is a protection over you and your calling.

Think back to a time when you asked God for something that He directed you away from. Maybe it was a relationship you desired, or to fit in with a certain crowd that seemed like it would make everything in your life better. Maybe it is a job or a specific career path that you thought you had to have. We have all experienced the letdown of not getting that thing that consumed our minds. How often has God been blamed for this letdown? If you blame God, then you must believe He is withholding something from you.

Psalm 84:11 tells us, "For the Lord God is a sun and shield; the Lord bestows favor and honor; no good thing does he withhold from those whose walk is blameless" (NIV). This means the thing you are asking for is either not good for you (at least right now) or you are not walking in His will.

Would you withhold something from your child because you wanted to upset them? We don't withhold from our children or our loved ones to hurt them. Quite the opposite, it is out of pure love that we don't give them what we know isn't best for them. Imagine that love multiplied by one million, and it still doesn't get close to God's unfailing, unconditional love for us. Aren't you thankful for His protective timing? If you haven't experienced that yet, one day you will.

The wrong crowd can hinder your walk with God and ultimately your calling, so thank God He didn't allow you to fit in. He saw something you didn't. That job falling through or the redirecting of a career path you had your heart set on was full of His favor and protection for you. The new car you dreamed about but never got may have resulted in a spiral of bad choices. One day, you will recognize you were not prepared to take that specific thing on or that it would have been detrimental to your future. As you experience spiritual growth, you will gain knowledge and wisdom in His Word and direction, which will help you understand how crucial His timing is in every single area of your life. Thank God that He loves you enough to say, "Not yet," or to completely redirect your desires. Growing closer to Him will spark a desire for His plan in your life.

CHARACTER DEVELOPMENT

When was the last time you had a conversation with your child during which you explained why something was not in their best interest? As I sit here writing, my daughter is just weeks away from turning eighteen, and the more conversations we have, the more I find myself saying things like, "I know you don't understand right now, but one day you will." If you have a teenager, I know you've said this recently: "Wait a couple of years before you do that to make sure it's what you really want. I don't want you to regret it." We were all told the same things by our parents when we were younger.

Why do we tell our kids that something isn't in their best interest, or they couldn't possibly understand right now? It is the same reason God responds to us when we are not yet prepared. If you were to take on a responsibility you were not prepared for, you would most likely be in over your head and the outcome would be less than ideal. When guiding our children, we often think it's age, but age is just a number. We tell them these things because they have not yet developed the maturity to make decisions on their own. Maturity comes from knowledge through different experiences. It's not about age. It comes down to personal experience and gaining wisdom. Spiritual maturity comes from gaining more knowledge in who God is, what His ways are, and who you are because of who you belong to.

I launched *The Covenant Woman* a year and a half before God told me He wanted me to start using my voice. There were some areas of my personal life that needed His guidance and my attention. He needed me to become more spiritually mature. Messages needed to be heard, some people needed to be removed, and more knowledge needed to be gained. He needed to prepare me for what He was leading me into. In other words, it was not yet time. I needed character development as He molded me to be more like Him.

As you gain spiritual knowledge, you are being molded to be like Him, and your desires come into alignment with His. He is developing your character through His Word so you are prepared for the assignments He has for you. If you are not prepared, you will make bad choices which are detrimental to you and those you are called to share God's love with.

For example, maybe someone is called to share their voice and love for God through singing. If they haven't gained knowledge in how to handle the spotlight and resist worldly temptations, they may allow it to go to their head and take away from God's glory through worship. As you grow, you take on His character traits and learn how to represent Him the right way. Representing Him poorly to those you have been called to serve could hinder their relationship with Jesus or even their acceptance of Him as their Savior.

WHAT TO DO IN THE WAITING SEASON

How often do we question God's timing? How often do we want things sped up for our own benefit? We live in a world geared toward instant validation, causing us to want everything the moment it enters our minds. When God's timing is not in line with our own schedule, we can start to question God. We may begin to believe He has forgotten about us, doesn't care about us, or is mad at us. The desire for instant validation causes many Christians to grow weary in the waiting season, which can result in giving up and not doing your part. We must remember that God always provides.

If you want to bear good fruit, being spiritually equipped is necessary. Wanting what God has for you must be the priority, as Scripture teaches, "For everything there is a season, a time for every activity under heaven." (Ecclesiastes 3:1, NLT). When things don't happen as quickly as you'd like or you feel like God's not hearing you, remember that He knows exactly what you need, and the plan has already been put into motion. Allow Him to lead you. His plans for you are full of protection, promotion, and favor for you and your family.

I think one of the most beautiful things about the Bible is that it gives us clear instructions on how to live our lives. Did you know Jeremiah 29 gives us step-by-step instructions on what to do while we are in a waiting season? Put those same instructions into action in your own life as you are waiting on the next step from God. The Israelites were disobeying God by worshiping idols and constantly sinning. They refused to change their behavior even after God sent warnings about what would happen if they didn't turn from their wicked ways. Because of their refusal, God allowed them to be exiled to Babylon by way of King Nebuchadnezzar.

In a new and unfamiliar place, the Israelites were full of anxiety and questioning what would happen next. Like you and I often do, they impatiently requested answers. Although they brought every bit of the isolation and consequences on themselves, there are three things God instructed the Israelites to do through the prophet, Jeremiah.

First, "'Build houses and settle down; plant gardens and eat what they produce. Marry and have sons and daughters; find wives for your sons and give your daughters in marriage, so that they too may have sons and daughters. Increase in number there; do not decrease" (Jeremiah 29:5-6, NIV). God tells them to do what they already know to do. He tells them to be fruitful and multiply while continuing to live. He tells them to live in His will.

Second, "And seek the peace of the city where I have caused you to be carried away captive, and pray to the Lord for it; for in its peace you will have peace" (Jeremiah 29:7, NKJV). Here God is saying, even in an unfamiliar place, take hold of His peace. He is letting them know He knows they are in unfamiliar territory, but His peace is still available just the same.

Third, "For thus says the Lord of hosts, the God of Israel: Do not let your prophets and your diviners who are in your midst deceive you, nor listen to your dreams which you cause to be dreamed. For they prophesy falsely to you in My name; I have not sent them, says the Lord" (Jeremiah 29:8-9, NKJV). God tells them to stop listening to false prophets and those who have been sent to deceive the Israelites. He is saying to block out anything that is not from God!

We learn the will of God for our lives by reading it in the Bible. Because He instructed the Israelites on what to do while they were waiting, you can take this instruction for your life too. Do what you know to do each day, take hold of God's peace regardless of the season you are in, and block out all the noise!

COMPARING YOUR CALLING

WANTING WHAT GOD GAVE THEM

Comparing your life to another's is something we all have done at one time or another. Maybe when you were little you wondered why most of your friends were able to go on vacation every year, but your family never had the time or extra money to do so. In junior high, comparison came from the way you dressed or the activities you were involved in. With adulthood came the comparison of lifestyles, and perhaps you started comparing career paths and goals with others. At some point, you have probably looked at another woman's life while thinking, "Wow, I wish I had what she has."

As women, we tend to lose ourselves in our families, daily chores, and responsibilities. When you see someone who looks like they are living an easy life, that lifestyle starts to look very appealing. Seeing that girl who is a social media influencer heading to the spa or taking off for another fun work trip while you're elbow-deep in your fourth load of laundry, you can't help but roll your eyes while secretly wishing you had her lifestyle.

It is easy to look at others, see a small glimpse of their life, and wish you could be like that person or have what they have. Social media has become such a tactic from the enemy for comparing our lives. It is important to remember what we see on social media is not an accurate representation of real life. Even the most "real" and vulnerable influencers do not share everything.

These social platforms can even make you feel like you are not doing enough, learning enough, hustling enough, or "Momming" enough. Watching what other women are accomplishing can sometimes make you feel like you should be doing more. Regardless of the life someone else leads, it is important to never forget the blessings in your own life. Remember what James 3:16 says, "For where you have envy and selfish ambition, there you find disorder and every evil practice" (NIV). Staying rooted in the Word and remaining close to God will push out the distractions that cause you to be outside His will.

ADMIRATION INSTEAD OF ENVY

Something I have learned in the past few years is instead of wishing I had the same talents as someone else, I can show my admiration for the gifts God created them with. I have a friend whose heart is to serve Jesus through being a missionary in another country. I can only imagine the opposing thoughts she had to take captive as she renewed her mind to what God said as she moved her family and devoted her entire life to serving people. I admire the love she has for our Heavenly Father and for others.

Another precious friend of mine joins her church every summer to travel out of state to serve families who are less fortunate. She and her husband, who are in their seventies, continue to do the Lord's work. I have never heard her complain, even while she is volunteering her time in the hundred-degree heat to telling others about the love of Jesus.

I have another very good friend who is one of the most servant-hearted women I know. She has a gift of boldness to share Jesus unashamedly with strangers. His love radiates out of her, and she brings a calmness to others in a way I have rarely witnessed. Earlier this year as she lay in a hospital bed after brain surgery, she was asking the medical staff how she could pray for them.

My favorite preacher to watch on television and listen to is Nancy Dufresne. The way she sits so calmly and shares so thoroughly the messages God gives her is truly incredible. Every word comes out so effortlessly and flawlessly. I am always amazed at how she very rarely even looks at her notes because she is so equipped and knowledgeable in the Word.

Pricilla Shirer's messages are so spot on and from the heart. She often starts with a story, bringing us full circle and tying it into her message in a way only she can do. Her delivery is always perfect, and she is such a passionate speaker. When she teaches, I can visualize what she is saying as if I am watching it play out firsthand.

I think the gifts God has given all these women are incredible, and there have been times I wished I could be more like each of them. But God has shown me that if I were to have the gifts He gave them, I wouldn't have the gifts He created in me, and He wouldn't be able to work through me to touch the lives of those my calling is designed to serve. Rather than trying to mimic a gift God gave another woman, I now thank God for the gifts in those who have touched my life and the lives of others. We don't just benefit from the gifts God gives us individually, we also benefit from the gifts God instills in others.

When you recognize how someone's God-given gift speaks into your life, thank them. If given the chance, let them know how their gift is making a difference in your life. Show your gratitude to God and those doing His work by becoming a connector. If I am talking to someone or a group of women who can benefit from the calling on someone else's life, you better believe I will connect the two or send her that way. This helps fulfill the greater purpose we are all here for, and I encourage you to be a connector of the gifts in others, spreading His love.

RUN YOUR OWN RACE

Focusing more on what God is doing through someone else than on your own relationship with Him blocks you from being able to hear His direction. When you are obsessed with what others have and hold grudges against God for giving it to them instead of you, you have entered the flow of envy.

Envy is not a fun trait to live with, and it is a sure way to hinder what God wants to do through you. Let us remember that envy comes from satan, and it turned into self-righteousness—causing him to believe he was better than God. God's character traits are found in Galatians 5:22-23: "love, joy, peace, patience, kindness, goodness, faithfulness, gentleness, and self-control" (NLT). Remember He brings forth fruit when you abide in Him, and His characteristics become yours (John 15:5).

Envy can come in a variety of forms. It doesn't just have to be wanting someone else's life; it can also be coveting their gifts and talents. Don't ever look at a calling God gave someone else and compare your talents or assignments with theirs. He gave you specific talents and assignments just like He did that person, and coveting the gifts of others is like telling God—to His face—that you don't appreciate the gifts and talents He has given you.

God's plan for each of us was created a very long time ago. Because He loves you so much, He made sure the plan for your life would serve your best interest while also advancing His kingdom. Each person is in a different season of life. We all go through difficult seasons of frustration and exhaustion. Remember that when you think another woman must have the perfect life. There is no one with a perfect life, but God has a plan for each season of yours.

Those of you in a season of singleness, use this precious time wisely. Spend this time getting closer to God, gaining wisdom and understanding, and finding out more about yourself by learning more about Him. You'll never get this time back, and as a person who experienced a very long season of singleness, the best way to utilize this time is by being close to God, studying His ways in His Word, and allowing Him to minister to you about your future.

For those in the season of bathing babies and telling bedtime stories, this precious time will be over before you know it. What you do now for your children will be remembered. The time you spend with them and what you teach them is part of being the hands and feet of Jesus. While you're making lunches at 5 AM, be grateful for the quiet time with God; don't take it for granted. You need His leading to represent Him in your home and everywhere else.

If you are like me, raising a teenager (or two or three), the love and grace you show them is an assignment from God. We are to be His examples so we can represent Him well. As we prepare these teens to be adults, we must set an example for them by showing them the importance of God's presence in their lives. The way we live our lives could indicate how they will one day live theirs, and it is never too late to put God first in your life.

If you are an empty nester or in the retirement season of life, don't spend your days wishing you could go back and live the days that have already passed. Change can be hard, but it's always more difficult if you don't have something to look forward to. What has God put on your heart? Have you said yes to what He has asked you to partner with Him on? His assignments await you.

Regardless of the season of life you are currently in, embrace the gift of God's presence now, and fellowship with Him about your calling. Not tomorrow when you have more energy, next week when the bills are paid, or on Sunday at church. Don't put it off until you meet the love of your life whom you've been asking God to send, or when the kids get older. The chaos of life never ceases, it just gets traded out with other responsibilities. It's time to embrace the call on your life, and to thank God for the opportunity to do so.

TAKING YOUR PLACE

HANDLING YOUR ASSIGNMENTS

No one can fulfill their calling without seeking God and saying yes to what He has called them to do. Colossians 4:17 encourages us to seek the call when Paul writes, "...See to it that you complete the ministry you have received in the Lord" (NIV). We wouldn't be instructed to complete it if it would be finished no matter what. It's crucial to the kingdom that you understand that the assignments God has for you will not happen without your pressing into Him and pursuing what He has given you.

One day when you have entered eternity in Heaven with Jesus, you will be asked to give an account of how you handled the assignments He designed for your calling. On that day, we all long to hear the words Jesus shares in Matthew 25:23, "...Well done, good and faithful servant..." (ESV). Can you imagine getting to Heaven and having to look into the eyes of Jesus, who died for our sins and tell Him you did nothing with what He gave you? Thinking of this makes me want to do better for the Lord and His kingdom. It makes me want to know Him more intimately, pursue Him more eagerly, and serve Him more joyfully.

We are here to serve Him and to invite others to know Him. Because we know this, we also know that this life is not just about you and me. It is about knowing, loving, and serving God by sharing His love and forgiveness through the unique gifts He has given us. God is not looking for perfection; He simply wants your faith. Serving Him is about being willing and obedient in what He has assigned you.

THE WAY TO THE HIGHEST BLESSING

There are too many people waiting on God. Are you one of them? He needs you to know that He is waiting on you. Being obedient means you are committed to His ways and His plan, even before the steps of the plan are known to you. It is an act of faith. When you say yes by faith, you will be filled with the desire to fulfill the call. God can't fulfill any of it if you're not in agreement because He doesn't make you do anything. After you say yes, His grace comes to fulfill those assignments through you. You will not receive further direction until you agree with Him. What has He put in your heart? If you are unsure, could it be that you haven't asked Him? James 4:2 says, "...You do not have because you do not ask God" (NIV). Get in His presence, talk to Him, and listen. In His presence is where you will get His direction.

Being obedient to Him stems from having faith in Him. Faith is believing in something even when your eyes can't see it. It is a decision to hold firm and stand on what God says, even when opposing thoughts and emotions are trying to get the best of you, due to circumstances you see with your natural eyes. Faith is your responsibility when it comes to receiving all that God says belongs to you, including your assignments. His plan is waiting for your faith to show up. Although your plans can bring a measure of good things, your obedience to God's plan brings the very best and the highest flow of His blessings. When you have faith, it shows God you are ready to carry out what He has for you. You will miss out on the fullness of His plans if you don't have faith.

Do you already know what God has called you to do? If so, are you letting something hold you back from doing it, such as a lack of finances, manpower, or resources? Did you know there's a supply for that and everything He is leading you to? Don't let "need" talk you out of what God has put in your heart.

His plan comes with complete provision which means He provides it all. That provision is only there when you are obedient and living by faith. The supply doesn't have to be visible. It's faith that enables God to bring things from invisible to visible. Move ahead in obedience. The supply awaits you when you obey Him, and His very best is waiting there for you too. Don't hinder the flow from reaching you by being outside of His plan—it will change your life and the lives of those around you.

MEDITATING WITH THE PLAN

In 1 Timothy 4:15, Paul says to Timothy, "Practice and work hard on these things; be absorbed in them {completely occupied in your ministry}, so that your progress will be evident to all" (AMP). This is clear instruction on how to handle the duties of your calling, and to meditate on God's plan for your life. Anything God calls you to, He has already empowered you for and He will fulfill it, but He cannot fulfill your calling apart from your agreement and action.

To be clear, the meditation I am referring to is not new age meditation during which someone is on a journey to center themselves. I am talking about biblical meditation in God's will and His ways. If they had spent time focusing on what He said instead of being distracted by the opposition, the Isrealites would have thrived in the Promised Land. They would have boldly stood up to the giants in the land just like David did with Goliath. Spending quality time with God will deplete the fear of what you are up against and what you will eventually face. It is crucial that you spend time focusing on God's plan for your life and allow Him to lead you.

When you throw yourself into what God has assigned to you, you are an example to others who are fearful of what God is calling them to do. We know everyone has been called to do something for the body of Christ. We also know that without their agreement and fellowship with that vision, the plan doesn't come to pass. Can you imagine how many people never fulfill what they were put here to do? Your saying yes, renewing your mind, fellowshipping with the vision, meditating on the plan, and taking those steps God gives you is changing the lives of other people. These may be people who aren't even affected by the plan itself but are inspired to get into action because you are doing what you're called to do.

TAKING ACTION

Knowing what God has called you to do is eye-opening, but acting on each assignment is life-changing—both for you and those who you are called to touch. When you learn what it is He has for you to do specifically, it can feel scary, nerve-racking, and way beyond your comfort zone. It should also feel exciting and joyous, as it is something that should be celebrated!

You get to partner up with God to do kingdom work, resulting in Heaven rejoicing as others start or grow their relationship with Jesus! Even one act of obedience to show love toward someone who may have never experienced the power of God's love, could change their whole life, which could lead to hundreds or thousands more souls saved. Every one of us is called to show that love to others.

When God first gives you a specific assignment, you will most likely immediately think, "I can't do that; I don't have the resources, intellect, background, or know-how." But if you could handle this with your own natural ability and resources, wouldn't that mean you don't need God's help? Do you recognize that when God gives you assignments, they are not for you? Those assignments are a way for God to work through you to touch the lives of others. Those who your assignments were designed to touch need to know that it is the power of God working through you. That's how souls are saved. That is how lives are transformed. No amount of self-equipping could prepare you for what God has called you to.

You are not to rest in your own ability but to rely on the equipping from the only one who can equip you for what He has called you to do (Proverbs 3:5-6). To begin transforming your life and the lives of others, you must follow these steps:

1. Seek God for your calling.

2. Await your assignment from God. (In His timing)

3. Say yes.

4. Prepare to be fully equipped by God with everything you need, including His provision and grace.

5. Act by taking the steps He gives you.

6. Rely on His Word, leading, guidance, and power. He is your source for everything.

Look at those steps one more time, and notice you say yes before God equips you. There is no need to know how, when, where, and what the outcome will be; you simply say yes.

First, He calls you, then, He equips you, and finally, He sends you. Each assignment God gives you with your calling is unique. He has a specific time and a reason for everything He does. So, when He sends you forth, remember He has already planned it all. Stay close to Him and block out distractions that will inevitably come as you are doing kingdom work. Allow the Lord to guide you.

God doesn't always send you immediately after He gives you an assignment. You may know for a while what you are supposed to do, but also that God is telling you to wait. He may need to teach you something crucial first, or maybe He is aligning something for whomever your assignment is meant to affect. Resist the urge to send yourself. If you take the timing into your own hands, you could abort the plans God has for whomever your assignment is designed to reach. When the direction from the Holy Spirit comes, act by taking the step He gives you. This is how kingdom work is done.

Don't forget: those you have been called to serve are waiting on you, and your obedience leads to theirs. By answering the call, there will be people who come up to you in Heaven and say, "Thank you for being obedient. It's what put me on the path to being here." The only words that could be sweeter are the words Jesus will proudly say: "Well done, good and faithful servant!"

WILL YOU ANSWER THE CALL?

Him: "Let's bring people into the kingdom, shall we?"

You: "Okay, God. I will do this for you."

AFTERWORD

The amazing and sometimes not-so-amazing thing about life is that ultimately, decisions about your future are up to you. Imagine what it would feel like if that thought that is constantly circling your mind was no longer just a thought. What if that leap you have been too fearful to take, or that idea you have been procrastinating over the last several years, no longer left your heart aching for something you can't quite put your finger on? What if you allowed those nervous feelings to turn into excitement for what God wants to do through you? Now that you have read this book, you know God not only has the plan but also has everything needed for it. I am cheering you on and praying for you as you advance the kingdom by saying yes to God's call on your life.

Answering the Call

Journal

Seeking the King and Advancing the Kingdom

SHAYLA JESSE

Answering the Call Journal is a companion to Shayla Jesse's book, Answering the Call. This journal provides a space for guided self-reflection as well as tools to measure your spiritual growth. It is designed to help you capture the changes in your mindset as you walk the path towards the life you were meant to live as a daughter of the King. With writing prompts that coordinate with the book sections, and generous page space for your thoughts, prayers, and scriptures, this journal is the perfect place to capture your thoughts as you Answer the Call.

ABOUT THE AUTHOR

Shayla is a wife and mom who has answered the call from God to write and use her voice to share His messages through her books, social platforms, podcast, and The Covenant Woman conference. She is passionate about providing guidance for women who are eager to strengthen their faith and say yes to the assignments God has for her.

CONNECT WITH THE AUTHOR!

web: thecovenantwoman.org

email: thecovenantwoman@gmail.com

Instagram: @thecovenantwoman

Tik Tok: @shaylagordonjesse

Facebook: @shayjesse

Facebook Page: @thecovenantwoman

Speaking Engagements topics include:

Grow Your Faith in God's Promises
And Take What Belongs To You

Say Yes To God's Calling on Your Life

Your Miracle Is On The Other Side
Of Your Obedience

Also:

The Covenant Woman Annual Conference
The Covenant Woman podcast

Review:

Now that you've finished Answering the Call,
I'd love to hear what you thought of it!
You can do this by writing an honest review on the
Amazon listing to help other readers find the best book for them.

We hope you loved Shay's book as much
as we have loved partnering with her
in preparing it for you!

We are inspired by her
experiences and guidance.

With a combined 20+ years in publishing,
we know how to help anyone
write, launch, and market a book.
So if a book is on your bucket list?
We're the team to take it from
brain dump to bestseller.

RebelQueen.co
marti@rebelqueen.co
Facebook and Instagram:
@rebelqueenbooks